W9-BHO-490

HAPPY ENDINGS
UPLIFTING END-OF-LIFE STORIES

LORNA BELL, RN, CHPN

LSTA # 07-226

A portion of the proceeds of the sale of this book will be donated to a hospice project.

© 2000 by Lorna Bell
reprinted 2006

The author can be contacted at:

Happy Endings Productions

(972) 745-8820   e.: loronbell@AOL.com   web site: lornabell.com
416 Kaye Street   Coppell, TX 75019

All rights reserved. No part of this book may be reproduced without prior permission of the publisher. Printed in the United States of America.

Published By:

Happy Endings Productions

ISBN   978-0-9700420-0-2

Photos courtesy of Broderbund on Pages 10, 90, and 128, Corel is Pages 70, 118, 154, Art Today is Pages 2, 114. Copyright 2000 Quality of Life Publishing Co. and its licensors. All rights reserved.

9000975539

Dedication

To the caregivers, those who have put
their lives on hold to walk someone they
love to heaven's gate. Praise is long
overdue for the well-spouses, the parents,
the family members and friends who face
the weariness and uncertainties of this
difficult, stressful, rewarding endeavor.
May your efforts bring you peace and
diminish your grief.

Acknowledgments

My warmest appreciation to my husband,
Ron, who believed in this project. And to
my son, Tom, for his enthusiastic support
and editing talent. Thanks also to my son
Mike and Thom Dohner of Encore Software
for their help with the cover design.

Introduction

In the Winter of 1997, my friend and colleague JoAnn Smith shared a remarkable story of an especially beautiful death. It was about a woman who predicted when her death would occur, booked non-refundable airline transportation for her casket, and was found decked out in a glorious peignoir on a bed of roses. This story had been told to her by another nurse, Cindi Martin, and it touched all of the "hospice hearts" who heard it. *(See Bed of Roses, p. 3.)*

I wrote it down and have carried it around with me since that day. The sharing of stories like this happens fairly often at all hospices. As I encountered other such moving examples in my hospice and personal life, I began first collecting, then soliciting, more sweet death stories. The number of stories grew.

This collection of end-of-life stories exemplifies the beautiful, hopeful side of a difficult, sad subject. Stories like these have been kept a secret long enough. Society should know that beyond the peaceful, touching deaths we in the hospice arena have come to expect, there comes the rare death that is so exceptional, or so filled with flair or glimpses of the other side, that it dwells in our hearts forever. And it cries out to be retold.

These stories share what those who work with the dying know so well. That we are here for a short time, that we are here for one another, and that the dying can be our best teachers of reverend, unique ways of concluding life.

This collection of special death stories is called *HAPPY ENDINGS* because these stories have the power to bring hope and insight to all who hear them. Could the sharing of these profound experiences challenge societal attitudes of dying, like childbirth has changed its image? Before modern birthing techniques and education, a baby's delivery was often a dreaded and painful experience. Now, we *celebrate* a birth, refer to it as a joyous event. And how very alike these two events are!

Beginning and ending. The newborn, like a person who is dying, is dependent, unable to speak or control bladder and bowels, and sleeps most of the time. Sucking is an important indicator of a newborn's ability to thrive. Loss of the ability to suck or swallow usually signals minimal functioning in the dying. Young babies and children often prefer to be naked and in a fetal position. This is an end-of-life preference too! The breath of the dying is called "labored," and it is quite similar to the cyclical breath of a woman in labor, who might also assume the favored, propped up, half sitting, half lying down position we often die in. The dying frequently describe a light at the end of a tunnel. Is this like the birth canal, with a bright delivery room light at its end? A newborn's heart rate is usually around 140 beats per minute. Most people who die gradually will also have a fast heartbeat, close to that rate. Many of my dying patients have exhibited a soft glow, and they begin to lose their wrinkles as a natural dehydration occurs, similar to that smooth, pearlescent skin of the newborn, so compelling and easy to love.

Birth and death can bring out the best in us. A new baby can turn a self-absorbed young girl into a devoted, sleep-deprived protector overnight. Being a deathbed caregiver is just as demanding. The big difference here is this: the dying have proven themselves. They have left a legacy. A life well lived seems even more deserving of celebration, then.

Those of us who have had the privilege of attending someone in his or her last hours find many common threads and truths, which seem to be universal. As these stories accumulated, they fell into the following five categories, exemplifying these "truths." They became chapters:

THEY CHOOSE WHEN THEY ARE READY. Some people know when they will die; others actually choose when their death will occur. "I'm ready," is a common statement. Death seems to be more a process that is allowed than something that happens to us.

FINAL GIFTS. Giving or receiving a special token of caring may be all a person needs to say goodbye.

MESSAGES FROM HEAVEN. Dying people spend time in both this world and the next. They enlighten us about the hereafter and bring us comfort. A community benefits from witnessing death, as it forces us to address our own mortality.

THE ANIMALS ARE IN ON IT. Many pets and animals in nature exhibit behavior that reflects their knowledge beyond our understanding of   them. There seems to be an abundance of stories where birds appear parenthetically.

ANGELS LEAD THE WAY. Angels often appear to the dying. They rarely experience death alone.

All who work with the dying have seen these truths repeatedly. We consider it an honor to be allowed to witness this final stage of life and to reap the wisdom, insight, and faith it brings. It is my sincere hope that these stories touch your heart as well.

LORNA

About the Cover

The rose is the symbol of love. A pink rose means
gratitude. Both are emotions we feel toward our
teachers, the souls who have taught us so much
about life's conclusion.

Hearing the first story, *Bed of Roses*, sparked my
passion for collecting these stories. I didn't know it
yet, but this book had been conceived.

It's been a labor of love.

This rose is a tribute to that first lady in *Bed of
Roses*, to all the other souls reflected on these
pages, and to the contributors who have generously
shared their stories.

Table of Contents

Chapter Three: *Messages From Heaven*

Chapter Four: *The Animals Are In On It*

Chapter Five: *Angels Lead the Way*

CHAPTER ONE

THEY CHOOSE
WHEN THEY ARE READY

Some people know when they will die.
Others actually choose when their death will occur.
"I'm ready," is a common statement. Death seems to
be more a process that is *allowed* than something
that *happens* to us.

HAPPY ENDINGS

ℬ𝓔𝓓 of ℛ𝓞𝓢𝓔𝓢

"This is what I will be wearing when I die," my patient stated as she held up a beautiful blue Dior peignoir. In my years as a hospice nurse, most of my patients wore diapers, hospital gowns, even "birthday suits," but I had never seen anyone wearing such an exquisite gown.

One day, this patient told her daughter that she was in the presence of her departed husband. She said it was a private conversation, and she wanted to be alone with him. The daughter asked if she could stay, but the mother insisted on privacy. The mother said that she and her husband had much to share in a short time. The daughter honored her mother's wishes.

This happened on a Tuesday, and the mother later explained that her husband would be back and that she would be "going home" with him on Sunday. Throughout the week she kept asking her daughter, "Is it Sunday yet?"

Photo courtesy of Donna Hall

When Sunday arrived, the patient urged family members to leave for work as usual. Then she asked her son-in-law to buy her some roses and carnations. She also wanted him to bring the other flower arrangements that had been sent to her into her bedroom.

Her son-in-law returned at 2 p.m. with her flowers, and she asked to be by herself.

Thinking she was resting, her family didn't check on her until 6:15 p.m. They found her lying on a bed of roses, flower petals and flickering candles surrounding her, and she was wearing a radiant smile and her elegant blue Dior gown. Her rosary was in her hands.

The family later learned that their mother had prearranged for an airline ticket for the next day, so her casket could be transported. The destination? The city where her husband was buried. She wanted to be laid to rest by his side in her beautiful blue gown, on a bed of roses.

Cyndi Martin,
Georgia Cancer Specialists

"It is not strange that early love of the heart should come back, as it so often does when the dim eye is brightening with its last light. It is not strange that the freshest fountains the heart has ever known in its wastes should bubble up anew when the lifeblood is growing stagnant. It is not strange that a bright memory should come to a dying old man, as the sunshine breaks across the hills at the close of a stormy day; nor that in the light of that ray, the very clouds that made the day dark should grow gloriously beautiful."

- *Hawthorne*

HAPPY ENDINGS

𝒯HE JOKESTER

"I'm a jokester," Bill said several times during his morning admission to our in-patient hospice. Bill loved to talk, so his admission took several hours longer than usual. Each question reminded him of a story or a joke, and when Bill held court, he couldn't and wouldn't be hurried. He was especially proud of the black book he had started in 1938. It was filled with his favorite jokes.

When Bill's family and friends went out for lunch, he shared his master plan with me. He wanted me to advise his children that he had set a time, a deadline as he called it, after which he would receive no visitors. He wanted everyone to say goodbye, and then to leave him alone to concentrate on dying.

Many of his family members and friends were coming from out-of-town, and some were flying in that night. Bargaining for the children, I

Photo courtesy of Dreamtime.com

suggested a deadline of five days. Bill shook his head "no." "Two days?" I asked. He shook his head "no" again, and replied, "eight o'clock tonight." I warned Bill that he was looking pretty good, and he might not be able to die that quickly, even with peace and quiet and concentration. After I agreed to relate his wishes to the family, Bill told me his favorite risque joke to cheer me up.

Bill's family accepted his deadline and said their goodbyes. They were gone by 8 p.m. that night. At 10 p.m., an out-of-town relative who did not know about the deadline came in. I checked Bill's room, but we didn't disturb him, as he appeared to be fast asleep or deeply concentrating.

Several hours later, Bill died peacefully in his sleep.

Leslie Ware,
Hospice Atlanta

"He searched for his accustomed fear
of death and could not find it."

- Leo Tolstoy
(from The Death of Ivan Ilyich)

℘AT'S FAREWELL

"I'm dying, and I want to see and talk to everyone. And I want you to spoil me rotten."

When my patient, Pat, heard she was terminal, she called her family and friends together for a celebration. Everyone she knew and loved came to joke, laugh, and be with her. The family had a video camera, and they recorded the stories she told. They ate all of her favorite foods: lobster, London broil, and strawberries dipped in chocolate. She selected gifts of her fondest things from the house, and wrapped them with care for her children and grandchildren. She took the time to write letters to everyone she knew and loved. She put them in a stack and asked that they not be opened until she had died.

On Saturday, she told her friends to go home. Her kids stayed and partied with her, sitting around in their pajamas, drinking beer all night,

Photo by Broderbund

eating junk food, and laughing. After Sunday breakfast, she said she was really tired, and she went to bed. Pat never woke up. On Tuesday, with her kids all around her, she took her last breath, and died peacefully.

Pat had prepared her family for her passing. She left directions that she be cremated in her pink chiffon negligee and the black cowboy boots she had loved but hadn't worn, because they hurt her feet. Instead of a funeral, her family had instructions to have a huge barbecue on their property. They hung her ashes in a birdfeeder up in a tree, to "fly" out over the land during the celebration of her life.

Afterward, everyone came into the house and opened their presents and letters. Pat's death was so peaceful, and her children were so well prepared, that her end was not at all tragic, but a grand finale to a beautiful life.

Kristin Griffin,
Hospice Atlanta

"Be still prepared for death; and death or
life shall thereby be the sweeter."

- *Shakespeare*

HAPPY ENDINGS

𝒯HE WEIGH-IN

Most of our patients begin to lose weight as they approach death and often are distressed by their loss of body mass, strength, and stamina. But I had one patient who eagerly anticipated her daily weigh-in. Not until she reached her goal weight of 107 pounds did I understand the reasoning behind her delight at wasting away.

Beaming from ear to ear, she stepped down fom the scales and reported, "Now, I'm finally ready." She explained that she weighed 107 pounds when she was a young bride. Her goal was to be wearing her wedding dress when she was reunited with her husband, who had died

Photo by Dreamstime

several years before. For that special reunion, she looked forward to being "the same size I was when we were married."

She died shortly after that and was buried in her wedding gown—a perfect fit.

Betty De Jesus,
Southwest Christian Hospice

"Come death, if you will: you cannot divide us; you can only unite us."

- *Franz Grillparzer*

HAPPY ENDINGS

Special Delivery

Mona was not going to talk about her lung cancer, take any medication, or use oxygen. "I'm okay!" she would say during our weekly visits. It was unclear who she was trying to convince, herself or me. As her social worker, I found her in worrisome states of neglect each visit. Mona's lung cancer had been diagnosed quite by accident, when she fell and was x-rayed for fractures.

Mona had been the wife of an Army Chaplain, the mother of three grown sons, and had traveled around the world. Now, Mona was engulfed in fear and denial, and she was resistant to offers of help. Consequently, she had become a recluse in her own home, never venturing out. She sat in her chair, drank her Jim Beam, and smoked her cigarettes. She reflected on a life that included adultery, pondering what punishment God had in store for her.

Photo by Dwight Flegel

Over time, the family hired a sitter, Margaret, who was both kind and tolerant. Mona and Margaret hit it off, and my concerns about Mona's neglect were resolved. As Mona's health declined, Margaret managed her weakness and loss of control with great patience. As the moment of death neared, Mona began the breathing that heralds the end, and Margaret called our agency for help.

Meanwhile, Mona's priest, who had been driving by, stopped in just in time to give her the Last Sacrament. As he and Margaret began lifting her from the wheelchair, Mona breathed her last breath.

How ironic that the woman who feared God and His punishment was delivered to His home in the arms of one of His servants!

Suzanne LaFrambois,
Hospice Atlanta

"Some people make their own epitaphs,
and bespeak the reader's goodwill. It
were, indeed, to be wished that every man
would early learn in this manner to make his
own, and that he would draw it up in terms
as flattering as possible, and he would
make it the employment of his whole life to
deserve it."

- *Goldsmith*

HAPPY ENDINGS

ℒIGHT THE WAY HOME

My mom was diagnosed with dementia when she was in her 80s. She was very forgetful, but remained physically active.

Mom was a talented pianist. If someone named a song and asked her to play it, she couldn't. But if they hummed the same song, she could play it from "memory."

As she grew older, her forgetfulness worsened, and she began to wander. She would slip away and get lost. Finally, it got so bad that we had to put her in the Sisters' Convalescent Home.

Her wandering at the Convalescent Home continued, and she would often visit the night nurses' desk as she walked about the building. To help her find her way back to her room, Sister Carol devised a way to guide her. She left a lamp on in the doorway of Mom's room, which Mom could see from far away.

Photo by Dwight Flegel

When Mother became sicker, she told us that she was ready to die, but, for some reason, she didn't. Sister Carol suggested that maybe she needed to be led "home." That night, after Mom was in bed, Sister Carol slipped in and turned out the light. Mom died that night.

Larry Crisler,
Son and Caregiver

"When we walk to the edge of all the light we have and take a step into the darkness of the unknown, we must believe one of two things will happen - there will be something solid for us to stand upon, or we will be taught to fly."

- Anonymous

HAPPY ENDINGS

$\mathscr{D}$YING TO GET TO TEXAS

When we admitted our patient with lung cancer to our home hospice program, he told us of his plans to "make the rounds" to see his many kids. He wanted to say his goodbyes by traveling with his wife across the country in their van. Born and raised in Amarillo, Texas, he was determined to die "at home" on Texas soil. Naturally, we called him Tex.

I checked Tex's health status before their departure and found his condition had worsened. We explained that he would need to leave immediately if he hoped to drive to Texas, as his health was quite poor. Tex had become oxygen dependent, so Tim, one of the delivery guys, made oxygen holders for the cylinders in the van. We made arrangements to replenish his oxygen supply along the way. However, Tex was deteriorating very quickly. It became apparent that he had, at most, a few days to live. The road trip was cancelled and flight plans were made with Delta Airlines,

Photo by Dreamstime

with oxygen on board. There were impediments at each step. Tex would have to change planes in Dallas. Then, on the day he left, it snowed in Atlanta. Because snow is so rare in Atlanta, some flights were cancelled. We breathed a huge sigh of relief as his plane took off.

During the flight, his wife kept saying, "Honey, we are almost there. We'll be home soon."

He was at death's door when his daughter's station wagon met them on the tarmac at the Amarillo airport. Tex had to be lifted into the waiting car. His wife said to him, "Honey, we're home ! We're in Texas!"

Tex said, "Thank you," and died.

Lee Ann Henderson,
Hospice Atlanta

"You know, if we were to put this apple down and leave it, it would be spoiled, gone in a few days. But if we were to take a bite of it... like this... it would become part of us, and we would take it with us forever. Everything is on its way somewhere... Everything."

- George Malley, Phenomenon

ᏙWO BY TWO

Photo by Dwight Flegel

My Great Aunt Ida Mae and Uncle Chris lived in a little cabin out in the bayou near Monroe, Louisiana. They had been sweethearts for over 55 years. My uncle had some health problems and became too much for my Aunt Ida Mae to handle. She had to put him in a nursing home, but she spent every day with him, until she developed an aneurysm. She was hospitalized for two weeks. They were not used to being apart, and two weeks seemed like a long time.

When Ida Mae was discharged from the hospital, she drove to the nursing home and brought Uncle Chris back to their little cedar cabin in the swamp. They apparently sat down on the couch together and put their arms around each other like old times. That's how we found them—in each other's arms. Aunt Ida Mae had died suddenly of complications from the aneurysm repair, and the coroner said Uncle Chris must have died at almost the same time. It was easier for us kids to face their deaths knowing they were knocking at heaven's door together.

Will Reid,
Family Member

"A coincidence is a small miracle where God chose to remain anonymous."

- *Heidi Quade*

CHAPTER TWO

FINAL GIFTS

Giving or receiving a special token of caring
may be all a person needs to say goodbye.

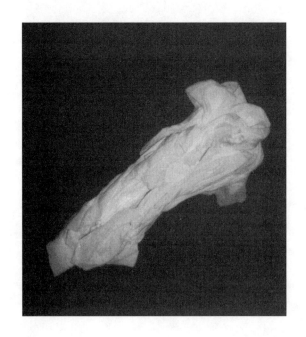

HAPPY ENDINGS

Angel in My Hand

Photo courtesy of Delores Mercer. Retouched by Dwight Flegel.

My father was in the hospital and had been told he was about to lose his battle with pancreatic cancer. It had quickly spread to his lungs and throughout his abdomen, causing him severe pain.

Daddy was an old John Wayne lookalike, a west Texas cowboy who loved people. But he had grown quiet and accepting, and he slept much of the time.

I was sitting with him at the hospital after his surgery. Other family members had arrived to take their turn. I put on my coat and woke him, taking his hand to say goodbye for the night. He held my hand tightly, as though he didn't want me to leave. He talked as though he was saying goodbye forever, and I was alarmed and began to cry. Daddy pulled me close and whispered that he had just been to heaven and back, and that he was ready. As I cried, he tried to console me, saying, "Do you see what I have in my hand?"

There was a tissue sticking out of his other fist, and I said, "You asked me for a Kleenex, Daddy. There's a Kleenex in your hand."

"No, no, open my hand. See, there's an angel!"

As I pried open his free hand, there, in his palm, lay the perfect likeness of a tissue-paper angel, with a face, dress and wings! He could not have fashioned it himself, as I had been holding his other hand.

My father died a few days later. I have kept his angel, as it brings me comfort. After all, how could a man with an angel in his hand not be all right? I have lovingly placed this angel in a frame, along with Daddy's saying: *He shall give His Angels charge over thee that they keep thee in all thy ways.* (Ps 90:11)

> *Delores Mercer,*
> *Daughter and Caregiver*

"We are not human beings having a spiritual experience. We are spiritual beings having a human experience."

- Teilhard de Chardin

HAPPY ENDINGS

Ᏸuffy's Ꮡainbow

My friend, Pat, had an eight-year-old daughter named Buffy. One day this little girl went for a bike ride with her friends and was hit by a car. She was seriously injured and, after two days, Pat allowed the doctors to remove the little girl's life support. Buffy was dead.

Devastated and exhausted, Pat went home. She found herself drawn to Buffy's room. On Buffy's desk, Pat found a recent story Buffy had written and illustrated.

The story was about a woman who had died and gone to heaven. She discovered that heaven was more beautiful than anyone could imagine. She wanted to let the world know what they had to look forward to. She could not think of a way to tell her loved ones, and she began to cry. Her tears became rainbows and fell to earth in a myriad of colors. People came running outside and rejoiced at the sight. The woman was happy.

Photo by Dreamstime

Buffy had drawn a beautiful picture of rainbows, rejoicing people, and a woman's face in the clouds, smiling with joy. Buffy's Mom felt that her little girl somehow knew she was going to die and left the drawing and story to comfort her.

Buffy's family members and friends heard about the story and brought balloon bouquets to the funeral. At the grave site, all the balloons were released at once into the afternoon sky. Buffy would have said it looked like a giant rainbow.

Candace Pokerney,

Community Hospice of Northeast Florida

A person's a person no matter
how small."

- Dr. Seuss

HAPPY ENDINGS

ᴅAVID'S GIFTS

David was at dinner when I arrived to have him sign revocation papers to discontinue our home hospice services. This would enable him to receive 24-hour care as a patient at an inpatient facility. "This place is going to be the ticket," he reported. David had been handsome, wealthy and worldly, but now he was frail, penniless, and losing his struggle with AIDS.

We were sad to terminate our relationship, and he asked me to move his wheelchair outside so we could talk. We sat on the deck, watching the city lights, and he began his "gifts."

"You ladies are classy," he began. "You don't have to do this. I'm not your client anymore. Let me tell you, I appreciate you. It's what makes this experience palatable." He began bequeathing compliments.

"Lorna. I liked her pertness, her femininity without being prissy,

Photo by Dreamstime

her frosting.

"You. Well, you were going to *have* to be good! Saying all the right words, with that comforting *voice!* So easy to sink into."

He went on, extolling the virtues of all the people who had helped him in his illness. They were generous, sincere compliments, seen with loving clarity, in our best light. "I'll see that she gets the word," I would say. I asked what he was most proud of. "I've messed up and done things I'm <u>not</u> proud of. I want them to know I left with dignity."

As I drove home, I was glad to have lingered with David for an hour that I could not bill for. I recalled my friend who had died from the same disease.

"For your karma, my friend," I whispered. A gift to us both.

> *Jackie Lawrence, LCSW*
> *Weinstein Hospice*

"I stepped from plank to plank so slow and cautiously; the stars about my head I felt, about my feet the sea. I knew not but the next would be my final inch. This gave me that precarious gait some call experience."

- Emily Dickinson

HAPPY ENDINGS

GRAMMA LIZ'S NAMESAKE

I first became aware of Mrs. Elizabeth Smith's need for a chaplain on a busy Thursday afternoon. She was an 87-year-old Catholic woman who had not previously wanted a visit from a chaplain. Now her nurse, daughter and granddaughter were all urgently requesting that I come to their remote little home as soon as possible. Mrs. Smith was very close to death and wanted to see me. I had worked an especially long, hard week. I secretly almost hoped she would pass away before my Friday evening visit, so I would not have to make the difficult drive in the dark.

On Friday afternoon the granddaughter paged me with another request. She had become reacquainted with her second cousin during their

Photo by Dreamstime

grandmother's illness, and their old love had been rekindled. She wanted me to come prepared to marry them in their grandmother's presence. After checking and confirming that this type of marriage was legal in the state of Georgia, I agreed.

When I arrived, I changed into my robe and stole and went in to meet the patient. Her eyes widened when she saw me walk in. I do not think she was accustomed to seeing a female clergyman! She seemed to think for a moment that I was an angel who had come to escort her to heaven. Then she smiled, and the bride and groom took their places.

The small family gathered around the bed for a short, sweet service. Grandmother Liz was just glowing, smiling sweetly. The groom's last name was the same as Gramma's, Smith. And the bride had been named for her grandmother, Elizabeth, so now she was a double namesake—Mrs. Elizabeth Smith.

When we went into the next room for a toast and some wedding cake, we heard through the baby monitor that Gramma's breathing had changed. The bride's mother asked me if I could help her remove some of the breathing secretions, but I told the daughter gently that this was of no use. I went to the bedside again and was just in time to witness Gramma Liz's last breath.

So we gathered around the bed for another short, sweet service.

This time it was a prayer to celebrate beginnings and endings, and the new Mrs. Elizabeth Smith.

Susan Bryant, M. Div.
Hospice Atlanta Chaplain

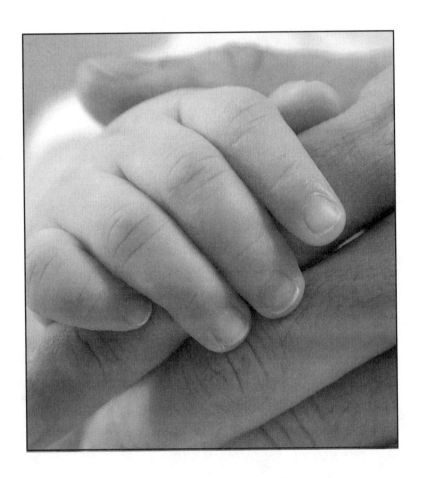

HAPPY ENDINGS

$\mathcal{I}$'M OKAY

Despite his obvious difficulties, my patient was one of those guys who would reply, "just fine," when asked how he was doing. He was dying of cancer, yet he denied experiencing any pain, nausea, or weakness. His wife would position herself behind him so she could communicate to me with a shake or nod of her head the true status of his symptoms. She knew he would always report, "I'm okay."

His disease progressed. One morning we found he had lost both his ability to speak and to move. His daughter came to the foot of his bed and gently asked, "How are you doing, Daddy? Are you okay?" Although he had lost almost all of his motor functioning, I saw this remarkable man's face light up, and he flashed her a dazzling wink.

His breathing soon changed to the labored stages of a dying man. Family members gathered around his bed, holding hands and praying.

Photo by Dreamstime

They reassured him of their love.

Our voices had awakened a little grandson, sleepy from the trip to Grampa's house to say a final goodbye. The child stumbled into the room, rubbing his eyes. I noticed our patient's paralyzed hand sticking out between the bed rails. When I slipped the little boy's hand into his Grampa's, a large tear ran down the man's cheek, and he took his last breath.

And we all had a sense that he was finally "okay."

Lorna Bell,
Hospice Atlanta

"Death is almost always
preceded by a perfect
willingness to die."

- Alfred Worcester

ᒪINDA'S DAD

So live, that when thy summons comes to join
The innumerable caravan, that moves
To the pale realms of shade, where each shall take
His chamber in the silent halls of death,
Thou go not, like quarry-slave at night,
Scourged to his dungeon, but sustain'd and sooth'd
By an unfaltering trust, approach thy grave,
Like one who wraps the drapery of his couch
About him, and lies down to pleasant dreams.

William Cullen Bryant

This is the paragraph my Dad memorized for an assignment in his high school English class. It bubbled up out of his subconscious memory during the last month of his life.

Photo courtesy of Linda Zwirlein

One day he told me, "I want to do it like this poem says, slip away in pleasant dreams. And then I plan to supervise all of you from above."

He died shortly thereafter, quietly in his sleep.

Linda Zwirlein, Admissions Coordinator
Hospice Atlanta

"We sometimes congratulate ourselves at the moment of waking from a troubled dream; it may be so the moment after death."

- Nathaniel Hawthorne (from The American Notebooks)

HAPPY ENDINGS

ℳEMORY LANE

We had a patient at Our Lady of Perpetual Help who was in the last stages of lung cancer. She was very sick, and she was afraid to die. Father Ed Murray visited her at her bedside, and listened to her confession. After talking with her, he said, "And now for your penance, I want you to think back and remember the very first time you were kissed."

Shortly thereafter, she died. The nurse who found her said she was wearing the most beautiful smile on her face.

Terry Gregerson, Hospice Coordinator
Emory Clinic

Photo by Dreamstime

HAPPY ENDINGS

ᴹY WATERLOO

Jack and I had a private joke about our first date. It was Halloween night, and we were in the back seat, on our way to a party. He tried to kiss me and I told him to stop. I told him that I didn't kiss on a first date. He playfully tugged on my hair, held my face in his hands and kissed me anyway. We always joked about that night. He called it his *Waterloo*.

Of course, we married, and spent many wonderful years together. Jack got cancer, and when it became impossible to care for him at home, we went to the hospice facility. I prayed, "Lord, I don't want him to suffer. If you are going to call Jack home, let it be soon." When I arrived at the hospice facility the next day, Dr. Booth told me it would be soon. I put my arm under Jack's head, held his hand and talked to him.

I asked, "Do you remember the first time you kissed me?" Jack slowly opened his eyes and I said, "We were with Gladys and Irving, in the

Photo courtesy of Novelyn Gobble

back seat, and you were stroking my hair. I said, 'Stop that, I don't kiss on the first date.' You said you were going to kiss me anyway, and when you did, that was your Waterloo!"

Jack smiled sweetly and squeezed my hand. I gave him a kiss as he died.

Novelyn, Wife of a Patient
Hospice Atlanta

"Those who love deeply never grow old.
They may die of old age, but they die young."

- Benjamin Franklin

HAPPY ENDINGS

℘EGGY'S

GOING AWAY PARTY

Peggy's doctor had told her she had less than two days to live. When I arrived on my admission visit, she had stockpiled lethal barbiturates, per the suicide instructions she read in the book, *Final Exit.* She told me she intended to take her life before her condition became painful.

Peggy was an accomplished and successful Jewish woman of 54. Because her ovarian cancer had spread to the lining of her heart, a rare but fatal rupture would likely occur. Peggy knew that this condition, called pericardial tamponade, would end her life after she experienced a few hours of cardiac and respiratory distress.

Photo by Dreamstime

I was sent to Peggy's home by her physician to tell her about our home hospice services. When Peggy learned she could meet her death in a pain-free, peaceful way, she agreed to abandon her suicide plan and allow a morphine pump to be attached to an intravenous line. This would allow me to administer "whatever it took" to maintain her comfort.

Peggy proceeded to orchestrate the grandest *bon voyage* party for herself I have ever seen. "I want to have a picnic," she said. From her bedroom she called family, friends, and caterers. As people gathered to say their goodbyes, she personally made sandwiches on her bed, handing one to each guest as he or she filed by. Her mother called Pizza Hut, requesting an "emergency" delivery. When a balloon bouquet with a "Get Well Soon" message arrived, Peggy howled with laughter.

She began giving away the special belongings she had accumulated over the years—a pin to this one, a favorite pair of earrings, a suit—along with a sweet statement about why each selection was just right for that person.

Peggy grew more breathless, and I increased her sedation as promised. She gave me lessons in what she called "being a Jewish Princess," ordering friends to arrange the sandwiches just so around the perimeter of the trays, with potato chips in the center.

As she lay dying, I told her that I had accepted her niece's offer to fly to the niece's home in Washington, DC, to help with the birth and care of the baby she was expecting. Peggy's eyes fluttered, she smiled, and I like to think that she understood.

Peggy's death coach was to be her niece's birthing coach...and life begins again.

PS: I *did* care for the newborn! The baby was born before my flight arrived, but I stayed to help with night feedings and new baby care. I was there to share in the joyful fun of being with a newborn. Peggy would have called it a party!

JoAnn Smith,
Hospice Atlanta

HAPPY ENDINGS

ᏝHE PIED PIPER

My mother was a determined, independent, New England lady. When my father died unexpectedly in 1941, Mom had to take on the job of raising two sons. Mom taught us the importance of work and responsibility. We all did our part to help.

Two of my mother's favorite things were kids and yardwork. The kids in the neighborhood would come over every day to help Mom in the garden. In return, Mom gave the kids lemonade and cookies and told exciting stories of her youth and her travels. She reminded me of the Pied Piper; everyone was entranced with her.

When Mom "graduated" into her 90s, her circulation began to give her problems. She refused to consider a nursing home, so she had an aide come to her house and do chores.

It was a tradition for me to send her plants every Easter. On the

Thursday before Easter, the aide called me. She said that Mom appreciated the plants but was disappointed that they didn't include a hyacinth, an azalea, and some of her other favorite flowering spring plants. Mom asked the aide to call the florist, order the plants, and then charge them to my account. The aide called me again on Easter morning to tell me that Mom had settled into her recliner chair and said, "Well, it's Easter and I have all my plants around me. It's my 98th birthday, and it's time to go."

And so, that evening, the Pied Piper died peacefully in her sleep.

Dick Scott, Son
New Jersey

"If of thy mortal goods thou are
bereft, and from thy slender
stores two loaves are left, sell
one and with the dole buy
Hyacinth to feed thy soul."

- Sadi

HAPPY ENDINGS

ℛoberta's Heir

I had just walked into Roberta's hospital room when she got the phone call that dramatically changed her life. I was to admit her to our hospice home care program. She had advanced breast cancer and was going home to die.

Roberta was being discharged to spend the few days she had left at home. The telephone call had been from her only daughter, with glorious news: the daughter was two months pregnant!

I felt such pity and compassion for this poor, sedated, gasping woman. With extensive fulminating breast cancer tumors over her chest wall, breasts and both lungs, fluid would build up and fill her lungs. It was one of the worst wounds I had ever seen. She was not expected to live more than two weeks before the fluid would return, ending her short life. It seemed unfair that she would miss one of life's greatest joys, becoming a

Photo courtesy of Lorna Bell

grandmother.   I wondered if it would have been better for Roberta to not even know of the new baby's coming, but I had underestimated the power of a mother's love.

Roberta told me she had faith. She went home, quit taking her pain medication, and prepared for her new grandchild. She dressed fashionably, and unless you helped her with her wound care, you would have had no idea of the involvement of her disease. To everyone's amazement, Roberta outlived her husband, who was several years her senior, and moved in with her daughter.

When her daughter went into labor, Roberta waited at home for the news of the new baby's arrival.

Roberta didn't answer the phone after the birth, and a relative found her in the hall on her back. They say she died very close to the time listed as the moment the new baby entered our world. She was a grandmother.

Lorna Bell,
Hospice Atlanta

With You My Child

Beyond your teacher's way, safe from their care
You hold a trace of each whose blood you bear.
Something of a lost ancestor's face
Something of a grandfather's lonely grace.
And when the night turns you toward your secret self
Learning will fail you and you will find yourself
The sum of those who passed their lives to you
And the same pulse I feel now will beat in you.
So, with you, my child, I will go
To times and places I can never know.
And after death has my life outrun
New life I'll have at the borning of your son.

ℛOCKIN' MY BABY

Photo courtesy of Ed Guignon

I was working at Southern Regional Hospital and helped care for an 18-year-old patient who had non-Hodgkin's lymphoma. She had been in and out of the hospital so often that all the staff knew her and her mom. This young lady was determined to finish high school, and we were all delighted when she graduated that May. In June, shortly after her graduation, she was admitted again. Unconscious, she was designated as a "No Code," meaning no resuscitation or artificial life support would be provided.

As she lay dying, her mom, who had always been at her daughter's bedside in the big leather recliner, was at a loss. What could she do to help her daughter now?

We placed the girl's frail, little body in her mother's lap. As the mom held her child, she began rocking and singing, kissing and patting, just as she had done when her daughter was very young. This is how our patient died, in the loving arms of her mother.

I was so touched by this passing. This is not the customary order of things, as we are supposed to precede our children in death. But if this is not to be, then what an honor it is to be there at the birth, provide the nurturing in between, and, with bittersweet love, comfort a child at her departing hour. This sweet memory was a gift to all of us who witnessed this final act of love.

Cheryl Mims,
Hospice Atlanta

"What would I want engraved on my gravestone for posterity? 'Mother.'"

- Jessica Lange

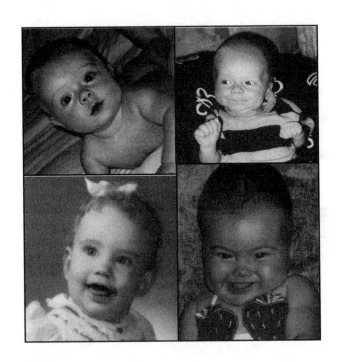

HAPPY ENDINGS

Surrounded by Babies

My patient was a 42-year-old gentleman with end stage lung cancer. He was in the hospital for terminal care and had been very restless. He suffered from labored breathing and "terminal agitation."

I entered his room one afternoon and found him awake, calm, and smiling. His mother, brothers, and sisters were standing around his bed, and everywhere I looked, there were pictures of BABIES! *Dozens of babies!* There were photographs and magazine clippings arranged around the bedside.

When I asked what this was all about, the family told me this had been his special request. He had been very restless until the pictures started arriving. Then he became peaceful, and his breathing was less labored. He

Photos courtesy of Lorna Bell

calmed down and was smiling in contentment.

My patient died a few hours later, surrounded by his loving family and lots and lots of precious babies.

Janet Lee, Nurse Practitioner
Georgia Cancer Specialists

"It is as natural to man to die as to be born; and to a little infant, perhaps one is as painful as the other."

-*Bacon*

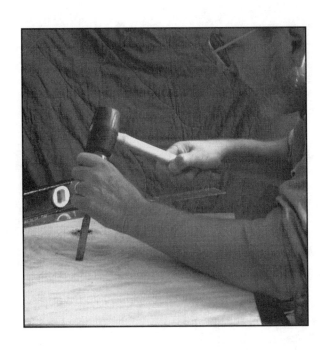

Sandra's Hope Chest

Lavar and Sandra had been married for 45 years. They met in high school in a little town in Mississippi. They married at 17, moved to Georgia, and raised a family. Lavar owned a construction business but stayed home to care for Sandra when her brain cancer became incapacitating.

When I met them and had been appointed as their hospice social worker, Sandra had become bed bound and comatose. Lavar had been attending to her every need. He was a man of few words, but showed his love for Sandra and his family by making beautiful wood crafts or furniture.

As Sandra's death grew near, Lavar began making arrangements to bring her body back to their Mississippi hometown to be buried. It was the town where they met, and where so many family and friends still lived.

Photo by Dwight Flegel

Lavar talked with the Georgia mortuary about transportation, and he was appalled to see the cardboard box they planned to use. Since the mortuary in Mississippi was providing the casket, the local funeral home would only charge a transport and body preparation fee, a minimal service. Lavar could not envision his dear Sandra going home in a cardboard box. "You have to understand what kind of person Sandra was! Her last words before she went into a coma were, 'Everyone should give their lives over to God.' This woman is my heart."

My next visit was five days later. Lavar was eager to show me how he had solved his problem. There was a beautiful cedar box in his workshop. It reminded me of a hope chest. It was custom built for Sandra and painted her favorite colors—pink and white. The inside was padded and lined with a pretty floral print. Lavar's Lady would be "going home" in a style befitting her sweet character.

I don't know which touched me more: Lavar's hope to champion his lady's dignity with this beautiful handcrafted gift, or Sandra's hope that "everyone would turn their lives over to God."

Monica Mitchell, MSW
Hospice Atlanta

"Life is eternal, and love is immortal; and death is only a horizon; and a horizon is nothing save the limit of our sight."

- *Rossiter Worthington Raymond*

HAPPY ENDINGS

ᏚPLENDOR IN THE GRASS

"I want to go outside," Henry told me. Henry was a long and lanky six-foot, four-inch patient who had been bed bound for a long time. To transfer him to a chair required at least three people. On the day of my visit, this 39-year-old gentleman was being cared for by his mother, his only caregiver that day. His sisters were all at work.

I wanted to help, but it would have been impossible for the two of us. As luck would have it, my husband had accompanied me that day and was waiting in the car. Henry and the mother agreed to allow my husband to assist, and we were all able to transfer him to his chair and wheel him to the patio.

However, Henry persisted with one more request. He asked to be taken onto the lawn. He wanted the foot pads of his wheelchair flipped up so he could feel the grass on his bare feet. I gave him a small branch that was near his chair, and he laid it across his armrest. "This feels good!" he said. It was a beautiful spring morning. The sunshine was warm. The dogwoods were blooming, and the air was fresh and fragrant. After about ten minutes, we returned him to his bed.

A few minutes after we left the house, I was paged. Henry had died. I couldn't believe it. Moments before we had left him smiling, lying in his bed. But it gave us such peace to know we granted him that last simple wish, to feel his feet on the grass.

Missie Edwards,
Hospice Atlanta

"Don't just count your years,
make your years count."

- *Ernest Meyers*

Chapter Three

Messages from Heaven

Dying people spend time in both this world and the next. They enlighten us about the hereafter and bring us comfort. A community benefits from witnessing death, as it forces us to address our own immortality.

HAPPY ENDINGS

ᏗMAZING GRACE

When Mama found out she was going to die, she said she wanted "no chemo, and no machines!" She made me promise to respect her wishes: "No sad singin', and no slow walkin'!" She said, "Linda, heaven is going to be glorious!"

Mama declined rapidly, and one day I came into her room and found her smiling. "I heard the bells," she said. When she told of the beautiful place she was going to, her eyes shone like stars, and there was a light glowing around her.

Later, the family gathered in the living room. I peeked in to see how she was doing. Mama said, "I thought I was gone, but He sent me back. I have two messages: "First, get the grandchildren to the 'Ark of Safety' as soon as possible. Then, call the neighbors, we're havin' a goin' away party." I believed Mama's phrase, "Ark of Safety," meant being saved.

Photo by Dreamstime

Friends and family came from all over, and the yard was filled with cars. Mama's name was Grace, so when we were finished eating, we all joined hands at her bedside and sang "Amazing Grace" and "How Great Thou Art," as she slipped away.

After Mama died, we were waiting on the funeral home. It was almost midnight, and we were all gathered in the living room. Suddenly, a car ran off the freeway and came crashing through the yard. The out-of-control car came to rest on the bank just over the roof behind the house. The driver came in to call a tow truck, and we looked outside. The yard was still filled with cars, and not one car was even scratched, and nobody was hurt! Now, don't you think Mama had something to do with that?

Linda,
A Caregiver of a Hospice Atlanta Patient

"Death belongs to life as birth does. The walk is in the raising of the foot as in the laying of it down."

- Tagore (from Stray Birds, CCXVII)

HAPPY ENDINGS

CATHERINE'S HAIR

Catherine had so much to live for. She was young and pretty, and she and her husband, Rick, had just completed medical school. They were both beginning long-awaited, promising careers when Catherine's medical check-up revealed a metastatic brain tumor. After an aggressive course of chemotherapy, which caused Catherine's lovely hair to fall out, she was told that nothing more could be done. Hospice was her only option.

Catherine was angry! This was such a harsh and unfair prognosis. She would allow our staff periods of closeness, punctuated by intervals of lashing out. Mary was her social worker, and I was her primary nurse. We found this situation especially difficult, because Catherine was so close to us in age and background. She was a constant reminder that this could happen to us. We tried to support this couple on their sad journey. Although the road was rocky, we eventually developed a close relationship

Photo by Dreamstime

with both Rick and Catherine.

One morning I awoke from a strange, but wonderful, dream. Catherine had come to me in my dream, and, with a great deal of energy and enthusiasm, she exclaimed, "Look, Cheryl! I have all of my hair back! And I'm well!"

Shortly afterward, Rick called. Catherine had died early that morning.

Cheryl Peavy,
Hospice Atlanta

"The gods conceal from men the happiness of death that they may endure life."

- *Lucan*

HAPPY ENDINGS

ℒEAH'S MOMENT

Leah was a brilliant woman who had immigrated to the United States from Germany during World War II. After raising her daughter, Louise, Leah attended Harvard University and became a full professor at a major state college. Leah's husband was killed in an auto accident, and the next year her older brother, Herman, died. Leah's grief masked her health problems until, finally, the family noticed profound confusion and memory loss. She had Alzheimer's disease.

It was especially hard for Louise to watch her mother's mind deteriorate. When Leah was placed in a nursing home, Louise became her mother's advocate, trying to ensure that her mother received the special care she needed. As the disease progressed, Leah became a nursing home based hospice patient.

As Leah's social worker, I focused my efforts on providing

Photo by Dreamstime

emotional support to Louise. Because her mother was severely demented, she was struggling to cope with the "loss" of her mother, as she knew her. Occasionally, Leah responded to music, so we sang to her. She eventually became incontinent and stopped speaking and eating. We realized that Leah's frail body was approaching death.

As often happens with Alzheimer's patients, Leah frequently appeared fearful and agitated. I worked with Louise to help her find ways to comfort her mother and to say her goodbyes. One spring morning, we walked into the room, and Leah was lying still. She was smiling. She became momentarily lucid and said, "I talked to Herman. He said everything is going to be okay."

The next day, Leah died peacefully.

Mary Stewart Hagy,
Hospice Atlanta

"The storm of the last night has crowned
this morning with golden peace."

- *Tagore (from Stray Birds, CCXCIII)*

HAPPY ENDINGS

Special Angels

Johnnie was a developmentally disabled young woman who had lost both of her parents. She was about 30, although her mental age was more like that of a little girl. She came to our hospice facility from a group home after her doctors discovered that she had a terminal illness.

Johnnie lived with us for over a year before she got really sick, and we all grew quite attatched to her. She used to say that, when she got to heaven, God would make her whole. One day she was kidding with me, and said she was going to look me up when I got to heaven and take off my wig. I would jokingly respond by saying, if God would make her whole, he certainly was going to bless me with a full head of hair! She had a peaceful death, and none of the staff will ever forget her.

Two years later, we admitted another young retarded girl, who had also lost both parents. Her name was Marsha. She had long, silky,

Photo by Dwight Flegel

blond hair and the face of an angel. Marsha was close to her last days, but she was terrified about dying. One day, she sat bolt upright in bed. She had been sleeping deeply for a long time, nearly comatose. She excitedly announced, "I'm going to be okay! I'm going to love it!" She extended her finger toward the room across the hall, pointing to room number seven, where Johnnie had stayed for so long. It happened to be vacant then, but she kept saying, "That girl across the hall, the one like me, she says I'm going to love it in heaven!"

She died peacefully the next day.

Betty De Jesus,
Southwest Christian Hospice

"We call it death to leave this world, but were we once out of it, and instated into the next, we should think it were dying indeed to come back to it again."

- *Sherlock*

CHAPTER FOUR

THE ANIMALS ARE IN ON IT

Many pets and animals in nature exhibit behavior which
reflects their knowledge beyond our understanding
of them. There seems to be an abundance of stories
where birds appear parenthetically.

HAPPY ENDINGS

BUDDY'S BUDDY

"I'm getting out of the prediction business," I told Miss Mable's daughter, Terry. I was tired of embarrassing myself, after falsely alerting the hospice team of my patient's "imminent" death so many times. My elderly home hospice patient had shown all the physical signs of being hours from her death, yet, she held on. One day, she opened her eyes and smiled at me, and said, "Do you know why I'm still here? Well, when the Lord is ready for us, He will eventually call us home."

The responsibility of caring for Miss Mable had fallen on two of the three daughters: Virginia, who commuted from out of state to spend weekdays, and Terry, who worked during the day. They were exhausted, taking shifts, and trying to keep their respective families and lives somewhat intact. This went on for two long months.

Miss Mable had brought her pet bird, Buddy, with her when she

Photo courtesy of Art Today

moved in with Terry. Buddy was an old, yellow cockatoo. They put his cage in the family room, but he made such a racket all the time that they finally put him in Miss Mable's bedroom. Buddy became quiet, and he was really a lot of company to Miss Mable.

Then I met the third daughter, Reta. She had been very close to her mother, maybe a favorite. She told me of an obsessive fear she had of being alone at her mom's bedside when she died. This thought terrified her so much that she had not offered to help out with any of the caregiving responsibilities.

At one point, Virginia was detained out of state, and Reta agreed to sit in the family room while Terry ran to the drug store for more medication. Reta had worked the night shift, and after getting her mom comfortable, she retired to the family room sofa for a nap. She was rudely awakened by Buddy, who was screeching loudly from Miss Mable's room. Reta hurried into the room to see what was causing all this commotion. She got to the bedside and took her mother's hand in time to witness her mother's last breath.

The family tells me that Buddy grieved, with a long period of not eating and uncustomary silence. He has gone to live with Reta now, and is back to his old cheerful self. And Reta has a loyal buddy.

Lorna Bell,
Hospice Atlanta

"But our machines have now been running 70 or 80 years, and we must expect that, worn as they are, here a pivot, there a wheel, now a pinion, next a spring, will be giving way; and however we may tinker them up for a while, all will at length surcease motion."

- Thomas Jefferson (from a letter to John Adams, July 5, 1814)

CARDINAL FAN

Each week I visited George, a patient in our hospice home care program, so I could monitor his terminal illness. George loved birds. From his kitchen window, he would watch them feeding. He especially liked the red cardinals. They were his favorites.

As his illness worsened, his three daughters brought him into our in-patient facility for around-the-clock care. His daughters were at his bedside as he lay dying. One saw a red cardinal just outside George's window, and they tried to rouse their father. They knew he would be excited to see this beautiful bird quietly perched on a branch just outside his window sill, but he did not respond. George died shortly afterward. His daughters were deeply grieved, and one was particularly bereft and wished she could just receive a sign that he was all right.

Shortly after George died, I was in his room. I looked out the window and the cardinal appeared again. This time, it was singing a sweet and beautiful song. I felt the family would find comfort in this coincidence. I called the family and they were delighted. Was this their sign? Had this bird returned to sing a sweet goodbye? I guess I'll have to wait to find out. I love cardinals, too.

Nancy Esker,
Southwest Christian Hospice

"The world rushes on over the
strings of the lingering heart
making the music of sadness."

- *Tagore (from Stray Birds, XLIV)*

HAPPY ENDINGS

ℱAMILY DOVES

My great grandmother Flegel had a cerebral hemmorhage. The instant she died, a white dove flew through the window, breaking the glass. It died there on the floor at the foot of the bed.

Thirty years later, my grandma Sadie also had a cerebral hemmorhage. When she died, a white dove, again, flew through the window of her room and died there. A loud crack was heard in the yard. When the family investigated, they found a large limb had broken off a tree, almost as though lightening had struck it.

The family felt that this was a sign that these special ladies were being honored. We fully expect my mom's death to be equally dramatic.

Dwight Flegel,
Family Member

Photo by Dreamstime

HAPPY ENDINGS

$\mathcal{A}$ Friend to the End

Frank's old bull terrier, Spike, sensed that life as he had always known it was changing. Months had gone by since Frank and Spike rambled in the nearby woods. Lately, Frank didn't even get as far as his front porch. Frank was weak, spending his days in bed, floating in and out of deep sleep with very little interest in their well-worn world.

The little dog had been Frank's friend and fellow traveler for 16 years. Spike was not ready to let go of his master yet. He pined by the steps waiting for Frank to come outside and take his usual seat at the end of the porch.

Finally, Frank's wife allowed Spike into the house. Once she let him in, there was no stopping him. Whenever the door opened, Spike would charge through, disregarding more genteel folk. Before anyone could stop him, Spike would bound onto Frank's bed, licking him awake, trying to

Photo by Dreamstime

put their life back as it was before. Frank sighed, blinked, ran a hand over Spike's flank, and passed back into deep sleep. Spike just sat there on the bed, wary that someone would prematurely separate them. Theirs was a bond that spanned decades.

Frank drifted into solitary peace. His hospice nurse reassured the family that love was the best medicine. They realized that Spike deserved a place at Frank's side. The nurse, kin, neighbors and the dog quietly waited. There came an hour when even Spike couldn't hold Frank back from his destiny. The old terrier watched, subdued, and slunk back to his usual place under the front porch as a long black hearse drove off into the dust.

Three days later, in the hot August afternoon sun, Spike waited on a curb by the courthouse watching the same hearse float through waves of heat on its way to the Baptist Cemetery. As the black van rolled past, the old dog fell in alongside. He loped two miles to the graveyard. The dog reached the tent first. Satisfied with his master's final resting place, Spike withdrew to the nearest hummock while Frank's family fidgeted on folding chairs. Spike waited on the hill, still as a statue in the blazing heat, until people rose to move about. Then he came down to join Frank's family members and friends, to give and receive the comfort that abounded.

Shirley Bethune
Hospice of the Foothills, Seneca, SC

"Patience and perseverence have a magical effect before which difficulties disappear and obstacles vanish."

- John Quincy Adams

HAPPY ENDINGS

Jane's Hummingbirds

Jane was the matriarch of a very dysfunctional family. Her husband had been abusive, and all four of her grown kids were struggling with drug and alcohol addictions. She was only 50, and she was dying of breast cancer, which had spread to other parts of her body. She was bed bound when I became her home hospice nurse. In spite of her sad predicament and many disappointments, Jane found joy in every day.

A major source of that joy was the pleasure of watching hummingbirds. The family lived in the country, and Jane's husband had enclosed the garage. He had installed several large windows, hung brackets, and suspended baskets of flowers from each. This beautiful garden room was where they had placed Jane's hospital bed.

It was there that Jane and I had our weekly visits. Jane always regaled me with reports of the many sightings of her beautiful humming-birds, but I never *saw* one! She would spot one, I would look, and *never* see it! I used to tease her, saying she was probably making these stories up. And she would assure me, saying that, "When the time is right, you'll see them."

One day she reported to me that, "The hummingbirds are coming very frequently, now." Then she slipped quietly into a coma. Her pulse became very thready, and, sensing that the end was near, I waited around. Finally, I went on to visit other patients, and then went home. I called the evening On Call staff, asking them to please let me know when Jane died.

The call came in an hour. I drove to Jane's home, where her daughters told me of my patient's last moments. They were both at her bedside, holding her hands, when she rallied. They said Jane opened her eyes, looked out her window and said, "I love you." They saw two hummingbirds at her window. Jane smiled and died. At that moment I looked out the window and saw two of the most beautiful hummingbirds I had ever seen. They hovered at the window, then flew away. The time was right.

Later, one of Jane's daughters brought me a porcelain humming-bird. She said it was one of Jane's last requests. Jane wanted me to have a hummingbird, like the ones that brightened her own life, so that I might see one every day.

LeeAnn Henderson,
William Breman Jewish Home, Atlanta, GA

HAPPY ENDINGS

Mama and Baby

My patient had been hospitalized due to a stroke when I met her. I was called to be her hospice home care nurse, if she became stable enough to be discharged. Her name was Sally, but everyone called her Mama. Mama had hoped to go home from the hospital for Christmas. She wanted to be with her family and, especially, to see her beloved dog, Baby. She missed her little companion terribly. Baby was 18 years old, blind, deaf, and she "dribbled." This caused the daughter who was caring for Baby a great deal of stress and inconvenience, but Mama begged her daughter not to put the old dog to sleep until she could come home and say goodbye.

Mama was discharged on Christmas Eve. Everyone gathered, including Baby, for a nice family Christmas. After the holiday, Mama declined rapidly. Mama died that week, with Baby in her bed beside her. Baby died the next day.

Photo by Dreamstime

Mama's daughter had Baby cremated, and she put Baby's ashes in Mama's casket. They had shared so much: their lives and their deathbed. It seemed only fitting that they share the casket and burial ceremony. Their headstone read, *"Love is as strong as death"* –Solomon.

Mary Ann Reeks,
Hospice of the Foothills, Seneca, SC

"Is it so strange that we want to meet again for the last time, to look at each other, to listen to each other's voices, ever so gently to touch hands?"

- James Laughlin (from "The Least You Could Do")

HAPPY ENDINGS

ᴍOLLY ᴀND HERBERT

Molly and Herbert were a devoted couple. My dad, Herbert, loved Molly, our family dog. The feeling was mutual. He always had a few dog biscuits in his pocket so he could give Molly a treat.

When my dad received radiation therapy for prostate cancer, he developed leukemia. As his health failed, he was hospitalized. He quickly began to fade. My dad had become restless and was in a deep sleep most of the time. In his confusion, he kept calling out for Molly. My mom was pretty perturbed. "Wouldn't it be nice if, once in a while, he would call my name, instead of the dog's?" she would ask jokingly.

Molly was getting along in years. One day, before going to the hospital to sit with Dad, Mom finally had Molly put to sleep. That day when Dad seemed to be struggling, Mom leaned over him and said, "Let go, Herbert. Molly is waiting for you." And he died.

Photo by Dreamstime

At the funeral, Mom tucked a few dog biscuits into his jacket pocket. Molly was waiting.

Mary Alice Farbotko,
Hospice Atlanta

"Neither the sun nor death can be looked at steadily."

- LaRochefouchauld

Photo by Fotolia

CHAPTER FIVE

ANGELS LEAD THE WAY

Angels often appear to the dying.
They rarely experience death alone.

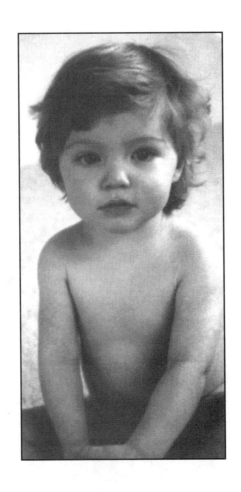

HAPPY ENDINGS

ℬLACK ANGEL

I had the sweetest patient, an eight-year-old little black girl. Her name was Elizabeth. She had been diagnosed with a particularly fast growing form of ovarian cancer. Every time I visited, her pain had increased, and her abdomen was more distended. She told me she was afraid.

Then she mentioned she had been seeing a beautiful little white girl playing in the corner of her bedroom. When I asked Elizabeth if she would like to try speaking to the little girl, she nodded. I told her I would be interested to hear what she might learn.

By my next visit, Elizabeth had gotten up the courage to talk to the little girl and had even invited her to come onto her bed. "Every night she tells me stories of how beautiful it is in heaven. She even brought her parents to meet me. And I'm not afraid to die anymore."

Photo courtesy of Lorna Bell

But Elizabeth was troubled. I asked her what was wrong, and she replied, "I haven't seen any black angels. Do you think there are any black angels in heaven?" I suggested she ask her friend.

It was Sunday when I next visited Elizabeth, and she was beaming. "They brought me a beautiful black angel with golden hair and golden eyes," she reported. "She was wonderful and so nice!"

"What did she tell you?" I asked.

"Tuesday," she smiled.

Elizabeth died that Tuesday.

Cyndi Martin,

Georgia Cancer Specialists

"All goes onward and upward
Nothing collapses.
and to die is different from what
anyone supposed
and Luckier"

- Walt Whitman
"Leaves of Grass"

HAPPY ENDINGS

ＤO NOT DISTURB

My gramma had a beautiful death. My mother was caring for her at her home. When my mama came into her room to change her sheets, Gramma told her she could not: there were angels sitting on her bed post, and she didn't want them to be disturbed. The next day she said the same thing, and she wouldn't allow Mama to make the bed.

Then she told Mama the angels had been telling her all about heaven. Gramma explained that there were lots of beautiful flowers in heaven. She said that she had spent time with her daughter, who had been killed at the age of ten. "Gertrude has grown up to be such a beautiful woman," she told Mama. She even said that her husband, Jacob, who had died many years before, was waiting for her. Gramma had seen Our Lord,

Photo by Dreamstime

and said that He was calling her home. Then my gramma went to sleep, and slipped away peacefully that night.

Shirley Bloodworth,
Hospice Family Caregiver

"Let death be daily before your eyes, and
you will never entertain any abject
thought, nor too eagerly covet anything."

- Epictetus

HAPPY ENDINGS

ℱ𝓇ᴇᴅ's Vɪsɪᴛᴏʀs

Fred and his wife, Sherry, had three children, and they loved life. When he was first diagnosed with cancer of the larynx, Fred left the country to seek alternative treatments. Fred was a fighter.

When his alternative measures eventually failed, Fred returned home and became our hospice patient. He had several wounds that often bled, and he needed high doses of medication to remain free of pain. Several weeks before his death, Fred began telling Sherry of his "company," whom he described as needing to be entertained. Sherry was puzzled, unaware of which visitors he might be referring to.

It soon became clear that these "visitors" were angels, who had come to talk with Fred about his death and what the "other side" would be like. These visitors were fairly constant companions, and Fred, as well as the family, came to know them fairly well.

Photo by Dreamstime

Red was described as the instructor, and Jamie was the angel with the light. They talked to Fred and took him "cloud hopping," as he called it. Sometimes the angels were simply there, providing comfort and peace.

Sherry learned to help Fred with his pain management by asking if the angels were present. He would look up to the ceiling and say, "Yes." Jamie would give him the "light," and Fred's pain would gently slip away.

The angels told Fred he would die when he was ready and that Sherry could take him part way. Jamie would then lead Fred the rest of the way.

Fred lingered during the last week of his life, wanting to be present for his birthday, and then for the birthday of one of his daughters. When he was ready, Fred died peacefully with Sherry by his side.

Sherry trusted that Fred, as promised, was safely in the hands of his angels.

Sharon Rugg, LCSW,
Hospice Atlanta

"To live in the hearts of those
we leave behind is not to die."

- Thomas Campbell

ℋE DIED LAUGHING

"He says Peaches is back." Mr. Earl's daughter had greeted me at the door, excited to relate the story. "He used to get so tickled when Peaches, his little dog, would want to go for a walk. She would put her leash in her mouth and run in circles around his recliner until he would recover enough from his laughter to take her outside for their walk."

Peaches had died 10 years ago. Now Mr. Earl was 87, and his kidneys were failing. The family hadn't wanted to discuss death with Mr. Earl, but he amazed them one day when he asked his daughter to remove his rings, "So the funeral home bunch wouldn't get them." He spent his days sitting up in his hospital bed, much like the position he had used in the recliner, holding hands with his wife, watching a big screen TV and, as he declined, dreaming.

As he deteriorated, he began sleeping more. He experienced

recurring dreams in which Peaches, with her leash in her mouth, would run in circles around and under his hospital bed. He began laughing all hours of the day and night. When he believed Peaches had returned, you could hear his delighted laughter filling the room with joy. Mr. Earl died with a smile on his lips.

One couldn't help but wonder if Mr. Earl's unusual dreams were the result of his medications or if the spirit of Peaches truly did come back to accompany her beloved master on his "last walk." Either way, the sweetness of Mr. Earl's last days will forever bring a smile.

Lorna Bell,
Hospice Atlanta

"Life is no brief candle to me. It is a sort of splendid torch which I have got hold of for the moment, and I want to make it burn as brightly as possible before handing it on to future generations."

- George Bernard Shaw

HAPPY ENDINGS

ℋEAVENLY HORSES

David had osteosarcoma as a little boy and, in spite of an above-the-knee amputation, it spread to his lung. He declined further chemotherapy, explaining, "I don't want to die sick."

The boy came to my care as a pediatric home hospice patient. As we developed trust and friendship, he and his mother began telling me about their dreams.

David said, "I dreamed I was on a big black horse, gliding over the land. We came to the edge of a wood, and we were standing in a river that had overflowed its banks. The horse turned sideways, stomping, as if wanting me to decide whether to go into the woods or out."

I asked David, "What did you decide?"

"To come out of the woods," he said. "If I had decided to go in, I wouldn't be here now."

Photo by Dreamstime

Then his mother related hers: "I dreamed of a Pegasus horse in a field, stomping and looking at me. I said, 'You are here to get my son. Go away!' And poof, he disappeared."

One day, David had just finished reading *Embraced By The Light,* (by Betty Eadie) and said, "You know, I'm ready to die." But his mother was not ready. She ran upstairs. Later, as she was beginning to float off to sleep, she had a vision. David came to her on his horse. "Don't worry, Mom. I'm okay, but I have to travel around the world to tell some of my friends goodbye." She said he was so happy!

She fell asleep and slept peacefully. When she awoke, she was sure David must have died, but he was still alive, resting in his bed. A few hours later, a friend from Japan called. He said he had just thought of David, and wanted to know how things were.

The next night, David's mom had another dream. "I dreamed David's horse and my Pegasus were in a field, with their noses kind of touching and nuzzling, as if they were communicating with each other. I began to realize it was time to let go."

That Friday evening David died, and I was called to his house. We were waiting for the funeral home staff to arrive when David's mom told me of another vision she'd had that evening. "I know people will think I'm crazy, but I saw this. I was in the kitchen and I looked up and saw David's horse. He had such a sweet expression in his eyes, and he gently tilted his head one way and then the other. I said, 'You're here to get my son, aren't you?' The horse turned and disappeared through the wall into David's room. I ran into his room, but he was still alive. I said, 'Your horse is here to get you, isn't he?' David said 'Yes.' I said, 'It's time for you to go.' And he died."

Reprinted with special permission from her book,

WHAT THEY TELL US,

by Nina Aylor, Pediatric Case Manager,

Hospice Atlanta

ℬ*rian's* Birdies

"Sit down, Mommy. I have something to tell you." These were the words my son spoke to my wife after awakening from his nap. My wife was surprised because Brian was three years old. At this time in his life, he spoke in short phrases. This was a long sentence for him.

A month before, Brian had been pinned underneath our automatic garage door for several minutes. When my wife found him, he was dead. CPR was performed by a neighbor who was a doctor. He was resuscitated, and placed on a respirator in ICU. His sternum had been crushed and he was unconscious. For two days we did not know if he had brain damage. But, on the second afternoon, he sat up, wheezing, and said, "Daddy hold me," and reached for me with his little arms. Now, a month later, Brian wanted to talk about the accident.

My wife sat down with him, and he began his remarkable story.

Photo by Dreamstime

"Do you remember when I got stuck under the garage door? Well, it was so heavy, and it hurt really bad. I called to you but you didn't hear me. I started to cry, but then it hurt too bad. And then the birdies came. The birdies made a whoosh sound, and flew into the garage. They took care of me. One of the birdies came and got you. She came to tell you I got stuck under the door."

When my wife asked what the birdies looked like he said, "They were so beautiful.. They were dressed in white, all white. Some of them had green and white, and some of them just white. They told me the baby would be all right." When my wife questioned this, Brian explained, "The baby lying on the garage floor." He went on. "You came out and opened the garage door and ran to the baby. You told the baby to stay and not leave." My wife nearly collapsed upon hearing this. She had knelt beside Brian's body, seeing he was already dead, and whispered, "Don't leave us, Brian. Please stay if you possibly can."

When she asked Brian what happened next, he said, "We went on a trip, far, far away. We flew so fast up in the air. They are so pretty, Mommy. And there is lots and lots of birdies." Brian went on to tell her that he had to come back to tell everyone about the birdies. He said they brought him back to the house, and a big firetruck and an ambulance were there. A man was bringing the baby on a white bed and he tried to tell the man the baby would be okay. He said the birdies told him he had to go with the ambulance, but they would be near him. And then the bright light came. He loved the bright light so much. Someone was in the bright light and put his arms around him and told him, "I love you, but you have to go back. You have to play baseball, and tell everyone about the birdies." Then, whoosh, the big sound came, and they went into the clouds.

The story went on for an hour. He taught us that birdies were always with us. We don't see them because we look with our eyes, and we don't hear them because we hear with our ears. He said you can only see them in here (he put his hand over his heart.) "They whisper to help us because they love us so much."

Brian continued, saying, "I have a plan, Mommy. You have a plan. Daddy has a plan. Everyone has a plan. We must all live our plans and keep our promises. The birdies help us to do that because they love us so much."

In the weeks that followed, he often came to us and retold the story. The details never changed or were out of order. We were amazed that he could speak beyond his ability when he spoke of his birdies.

Everywhere he went he told strangers about the birdies. Surprisingly, no one has ever looked at him strangely when he does this. Rather they always get a softened look on their faces and smile. Needless to say, we have not been the same since that day, and I pray we never will be.

Lloyd Glenn,
Brian's Father

"There are only two ways to live your life. One is as though nothing is a miracle. The other is as though everything is a miracle."

- Albert Einstein

Epilogue: Closing Reflections

We have learned so much from these stories. We have learned that, however painful the process of losing someone we love, there are many indications that some aspects of death can be joyful.

We learned in ***ANGELS LEAD THE WAY*** that we rarely die alone.

MESSAGES FROM HEAVEN stories have allowed us rare glimpses of the afterlife. We should believe dying persons, as they trust us enough to share their visions. These messages have the power to enrich our faith and to bring us more insight into what lies ahead.

Knowing that the dying have some control of the timing of their departure, as witnessed in ***THEY CHOOSE WHEN THEY ARE READY,*** brings a valuable lesson in our Lord's kindness. This could be His way of honoring one's last request to complete unfinished business.

FINAL GIFTS brings lessons about what it has taken for these souls to finish a last chapter in the journal of their life. Leaving a list of heartfelt thank you's such as those in *David's Gift* was so simple, yet the essence of sweet closure. My eyes were opened to a delightfully personal, celebratory wake in *Pat's Farewell.* This should challenge us all to do a better job of planning the conclusion of our own lives. Beyond that, being well prepared for our death transition could greatly improve the way we see our lives. Noting your after-death ceremonial choices would relieve an awesome burden on your family. Now is the time to express your preferences. Your family, who will be in shock, will probably be led to a traditional, expensive funeral and burial. The trend seems to be away from extravagant or goudy, toward more personalized, unique and dignified ceremonies.

I am looking forward to hearing from readers in other parts of the world. Do robins, rather than cardinals, appear at a death in Des Moines? Are there unique burial customs in Alaksa we could adopt? What have you learned about the afterlife journey of the soul from *your* dying friends?

Please let me hear from you.

LORNA BELL, RN, CHPN

"May you treat each day as a short life."
- Author Unknown

How to Really Rest in Peace

A grieving family is not prepared to comparison shop for funeral services. They are in shock, trying to arrange a large gathering to celebrate the memory of a loved one. They may be from out of town, exhausted, or overwrought. This makes them very vulnerable to guilt-provoking sales techniques.

Do your family a favor. Take a few minutes to make a list of your personal preferences, and tell someone where the list is. The following are a few points to ponder:

Funeral. The average funeral costs from $5,000-$10,000. If you do your homework, you should be able to find a complete funeral with a metal casket for $2,000. A frugal funeral can be arranged for $550.00. However, a funeral is not mandatory. Many people have opted for a memorial service at a *convenient* time when everyone can gather without the added stress of travel and job conflicts. If the caregiver is exhausted, the weather or time of year prohibitive, a more joyous time might be *later,* or on the anniversary of the death. Beyond this, choices to make in advance should indicate a religious or non-religious service, a private or a public service, the casket or urn present during the service, or just an old-fashioned party.

Casket. Prices range from $300 to many thousands of dollars, with an average of $2,200. Direct Casket delivers within 24 hours and can be reached via the internet at www.direct.com. You can also send for a do-it yourself kit for $499. That internet site is www.buildacasket.com. Rental caskets are available that have removable interiors.

Embalming is not necessary if the body is buried immediately or cremated. Eliminating embalming can save $500 to $900.

Visitation. If you have suffered from a long chronic illness, would you prefer to be remembered in your prime? Would you want an open casket? What would you like to wear? A video or photo album might evoke some sweeter memories. Hosting services at your home or church can also save your family money.

Burial. Choices include private, public, mausoleum/vault, or direct burial (taking the body directly to the crematory or cemetery with no preparation or services).

Cremation Options. Cremation costs about one-third less than a grave opening. Choices include cremation in a casket, cremation of remains only, urn burial, urn niche, or ashes to be scattered. A tip to save money: don't bury the urn.

Donation of Body to medical or dental school. Most medical schools require certain conditions. Prearrangement is recommended.

Donation of Organs. Some organ banks often prefer donations from those who are without contagious disease and who are under the age of 40. An exception may be corneas used by eye banks. There is no cost to the donor. Check with local agencies.

Music. Family favorites, "Our Song" type selections are growing in popularity.

Flowers. Have it your way! Or have a memorial donation, "In Lieu of Flowers."

Epitaphs, Headstones and Eulogies. See *The Book of Eulogies* by Phyllis Theroux, Simon & Schuster, 1997.

Wake or Memorial Service. "My friends should drink a dozen of Claret on my tomb" – *John Keats*.

Recommended Reading

Knox, Lucinda Page, MSW, and Knox, Michael D., PhD. *Last Wishes: A Handbook to Guide Your Survivors.* Berkeley, CA. 1994.

Lynn, Joanne, and Harrold, Joan. *Handbook for Mortals: Guidance for People Facing Serious Illness.* Oxford University Press, New York, NY. 1999.

Menton, Ted. *Gentle Closings: How to Say Goodbye to Someone You Love.* Running Press Book Publishers, Philadelphia, PA. 1991.

Carter, Rosalynn, with Golant, Susan. *Helping Yourself Help Others: A Book for Caregivers.* Random House, New York, NY. 1994.

Byock, Ira, MD. *Dying Well: Peace and Possibilities at the End of Life.* Riverhead Books, New York, NY. 1997.

Callanan, Maggie, and Kelley, Patricia. *Final Gifts: Understanding the Special Awareness, Needs, and Communications of the Dying.* Bantam Books, New York, NY. 1993.

Hutchison, Joyce, and Rupp, Joyce. *May I Walk You Home?: Courage and Comfort for Caregivers of the Very Ill.* Ave Maria Press, Notre Dame, IN. 1999.

Vitex, Michael, et al. *Final Choices: Seeking the Good Death.* Camino Books, Philadelphia, PA. 1998.

Bone, Roger C., MD. *A Dying Person's Guide to Dying.* American College of Physicians, Philadelphia, PA (www.acponline.org). 1997.

Oliver, Samuel L., Rev., BCC. *What the Dying Teach Us: Lessons on Living.* The Haworth Pastoral Press, Inc., Binghamton, NY. 1998.

Wheeler, Karla. *Afterglow: Signs of Continued Love After Death.* Quality of Life Publishing Co., Naples, FL (www.QoLpublishing.com). 2000-2001.

About the Author

Lorna Bell has been a nurse for 44 years and a hospice nurse since 1995. She considers herself a storyteller rather than an author. "Writing is something I do when I feel passionate about something."

She is the co-author of *Gentle Yoga: For People with Arthritis, M.S., Strokes and Wheelchairs*, which she wrote with Eudora Seyfer, a volunteer in the yoga class Lorna taught. This book was motivated by the authors' desire to make the benefits of yoga available to people with mobility problems and chronic illnesses. Lorna is also the author of "Rx for Burnout: Vacations with a Difference," published in the *American Journal of Nursing*. The article brought much-needed attention to global imbalances in health care in third world countries.

Lorna hopes ***HAPPY ENDINGS*** will promote death education and help to break the uncomfortable silence that often surrounds those concluding their lives.

The author lives in Dallas with her husband, Ron. They enjoy gardening, walking, photography, and visiting their four children and eight grandchildren.

Share YOUR Happy Endings

Beyond the peaceful, touching deaths we routinely witness as hospice workers, there comes the rare death that is so exceptional, or so filled with flair or glimpses of the other side, that it dwells in our hearts forever.

These stories have been assembled to retell the remarkable events in a collection called *HAPPY ENDINGS.* They have the power to bring hope to all who hear them. Could the sharing of these intimate, profound, and joyous experiences challenge societal attitudes on death, just as childbirth has changed its image?

If you have a happy death story to share, please jot it down and send it to me.

Mail to:	**Lorna Bell**
	416 Kaye Street
	Coppell, TX 75019
Email to:	**loronbell@AOL.com web: lornabell.com**

Submission of your story constitutes your permission to publish your story, along with your name. Please include your phone number so I can check my editing with you for accuracy. For confidentiality, please use first names only of patients or change their names at your discretion.

If your story is selected for publication, I will provide you with a complimentary copy of the book in which it appears.

Thank you for your interest and support of this project.

With admiration & affection,
LORNA

Quick Order Form

📧 **Email orders:** loronbell@AOL.com   web: lornabell.com

✉ **Postal orders:** Lorna Bell, Happy Endings Productions
416 Kaye Street
Coppell, TX 75019

Please send me _____ **copies** of Happy Endings: Uplifting End-of-Life Stories @ $12.95 each. Inquire about our multiple order discounts.

Also available at: Mentor Books, Amazon, NHPCO Market Place and Barnes & Noble by request.

Please send more FREE information on:

❑ Book Signings   ❑ Speaking Engagements   ❑ Seminar Presentations

Name: _____

Address: _____

City: _____ State: _____ Zip: _____

Telephone: _____ Fax: _____

Email Address: _____

Sales Tax: Please add 8.025% for books sent to Texas addresses.

Shipping by air: U.S.: $3 for first book and $2 for each additional book. International: $9 for first book; $5 for each additional book.

Payment: ❑ Check   ❑ Credit Card:

❑ Visa   ❑ MasterCard   ❑ Discover

Card number: _____ Signature: _____

Exp. date: _____/_____ Print name as on card: _____